TO:
Chase
Wishing you an
amazing
Happily Ever After!

♡ Taya Perry Miller

JOYCE PERRY MILLER

THE THREE MIGHTY PIGS

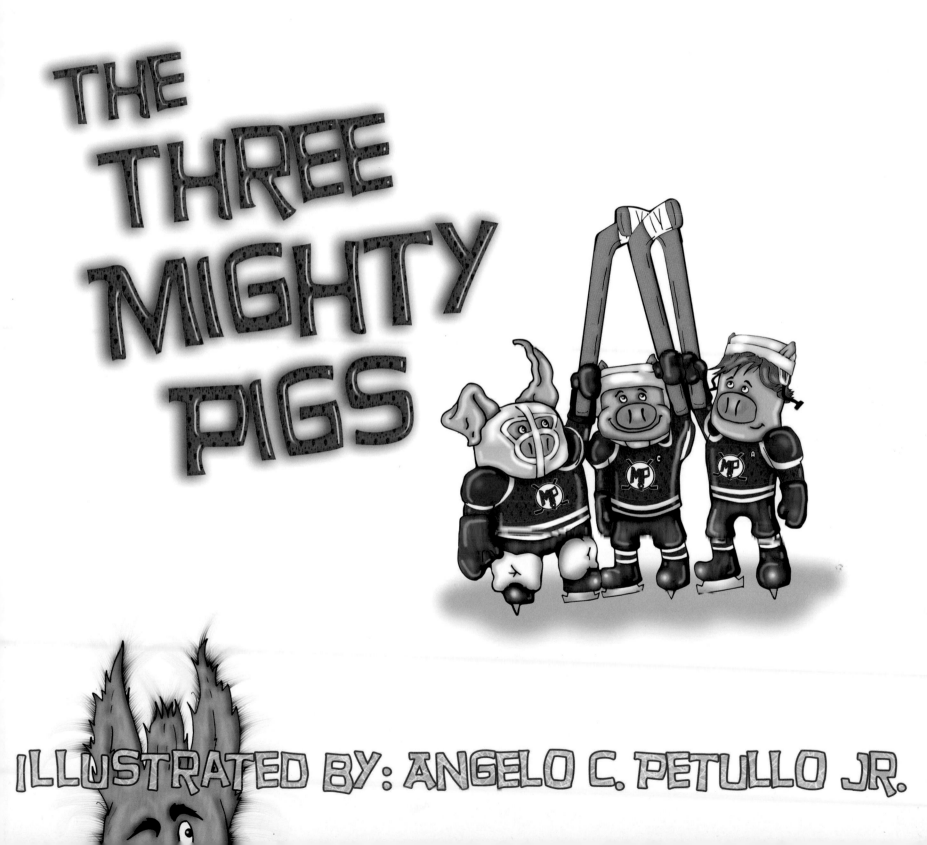

ILLUSTRATED BY: ANGELO C. PETULLO JR.

SPECIAL THANKS TO
BRIAN MILLER,
KERRI WAIBEL, SANDY MONTALBANO,
LAURIE MARTINKA, JEN ROETTGER,
JEANNE CASCIO, SUE DEBLOCK
& LYNDA VINCENTI

THE THREE MIGHTY PIGS

ISBN: 978-0-9968084-0-8

PAGE DESIGN & LAYOUT BY JOYCE PERRY MILLER

TEXT SET IN *HURRY UP* FONT

PRINTED AND BOUND IN CANADA

● FIRST EDITION ●

DEDICATED WITH LOVE
TO MY BOYS
TREVOR, AIDAN, & LOGAN

INSPIRED BY THE QUESTION:
WHAT DOES "HAPPILY EVER AFTER" REALLY
MEAN FROM A CHILD'S PERSPECTIVE?

THIS IS TREVOR'S 'AFTER THE HAPPILY EVER AFTER' FOR
THE THREE LITTLE PIGS AND THE WOLF,
INFLUENCED BY HIS LOVE FOR HOCKEY AND HIS BEST FRIEND,
TYLER, WHO INTRODUCED HIM TO THE SPORT.

ONCE UPON A TIME

THERE WERE THREE LITTLE PIGS THAT LIVED TOGETHER
IN A SMALL HOUSE MADE OF BRICKS.

THEY WERE FORCED INTO THIS LIVING ARRANGEMENT
AFTER AN UNFORTUNATE RUN-IN WITH
A CERTAIN BIG BAD WOLF.

AFTER THAT MISHAP, THEY DECIDED IT WAS BEST TO LIVE TOGETHER BECAUSE THEIR PARENTS HAD TOLD THEM ABOUT THE "SAFETY IN NUMBERS" RULE. BESIDES, THEY WERE ON THE SAME HOCKEY TEAM, **THE MIGHTY PIGS**, AND IT MADE GETTING TOGETHER FOR THEIR PRACTICES MUCH EASIER.

LIFE WAS GOOD
FOR THE THREE LITTLE PIGS...
EXCEPT FOR ONE LITTLE PROBLEM.

FROM TIME TO TIME, TYLER, TREVOR AND MATTHEW PIG
SAW THAT BIG, BAD WOLF LURKING IN THE BUSHES
BY THE Puddle Pond Arena WHEN THEY WERE PRACTICING.

THE THREE LITTLE PIGS WERE LEFT WITH NO CHOICE BUT TO CUT THEIR PRACTICES SHORT... AND BOY, COULD THEY USE THE PRACTICE IF THEY HAD ANY CHANCE OF WINNING THE

STANIMAL CUP!

ON THE DAY OF THE

HOMESTEAD SEMIFINALS,

THE **NEW JERKEY MIGHTY PIGS** WERE TIED WITH THEIR CROSS-RIVER RIVALS, THE **NEW PORK BELLIES**, WHEN TYLER "BRICKS" PIG SCORED A WRAP-AROUND GOAL. AS THE CROWD WENT HOG WILD, THE WOLF **POUNCED** OUT OF A BUSH, HOWLING LIKE MAD. THE BENCHES CLEARED; EVERY ANIMAL IN ATTENDANCE WENT *RUNNING* FOR THE HILLS, INCLUDING THE TEAMS!

THAT WAS THE FINAL STRAW
FOR THE THREE LITTLE PIGS!

THEY DECIDED RIGHT THERE AND THEN, THEY WOULD TEACH THAT
WOLF A LESSON HE WOULDN'T SOON FORGET. AFTER ALL, THE PIGS
HAD LEARNED THE HARD WAY –
BAD BEHAVIOR AND BAD DECISIONS HAD
CONSEQUENCES...

SEE
LESSONS
6 & 7

THEY WERE HIDING IN A TREE WITH A NET TO SPRING UPON THE WOLF, WHEN MATTHEW STARTED TO PANIC, "I JUST REMEMBERED ... I'VE GOT TO GO HOME!" "FOR WHAT?" ASKED TYLER.

"MAYBE WE ALL NEED TO BE QUIET AND PATIENT," SUGGESTED TYLER.

ALL OF A SUDDEN, TREVOR WHISPERED EXCITEDLY,

"OH, OH! THERE HE IS! LET ME HANDLE THIS..."

BUT TYLER PULLED TREVOR BACK BEFORE HE WENT TOO FAR OUT ON A LIMB.

"OH NO! NOT SO FAST, 'TWIGS', I'LL HANDLE THIS."

"HECK NO 'BRICKS' SAFETY IN NUMBERS RULE, REMEMBER?" GRUNTED MATTHEW.

"OK YOU'RE RIGHT, 'HAYSTACK', ALL TOGETHER, ON THREE, WE DROP THE NET."

SO, ALL TOGETHER, THEY QUIETLY STARTED COUNTING,

THEY HAD COMPANY ALL RIGHT.
FROM THE WOLF'S DEN, NINE WOLF CUBS EMERGED.

THEY STARTED SNARLING AND GROWLING AT THE
THREE LITTLE PIGS. THE SOUND ALONE WAS ENOUGH
TO SCARE THEIR CORKSCREW TAILS STRAIGHT!

"ME TOO," SAID TREVOR AS HE TURNED TO THE WOLF WITH SURPRISE.
WANTED
FUGITIVE FROM THE FARM
"YOU'RE A DADDY WOLF?"

"UMM... WHAT ABOUT NOW - ARE YOU STILL VERY HUNGRY WOLVES?" ASKED A CONCERNED TYLER.
KEEP CALM AND PLAY HOCKEY
"MMM, NOT SO MUCH - JUST HAD A BLACK HAWK FOR LUNCH," GRINNED THE WOLF.
"WHEW," BRIGHTENED MATTHEW, "THAT'S GOOD!"
Got Hockey?
"UH, NOT IF YOU'RE A BLACK HAWK," WHISPERED TREVOR.
Snooze Hockey

"GOOD POINT AND IT IS CLOSER TO DINNER TIME NOW--"

"--ENOUGH ALEADY!" INTERRUPTED THE FRAZZLED WOLF, "I WASN'T PLANNING ON EATING YOU NOW!"

"NOW? WHAT DO YOU MEAN BY NOW, EXACTLY?"

"ARRGGH! I'M JUST TRYING TO APOLOGIZE! I'M SORRY FOR ANY INCONVENIENCE I CAUSED YOU ALL."

SUDDENLY, THAT GAVE TYLER THE BRIGHT IDEA HE'D BEEN HOPING FOR...

"WE ACCEPT YOUR APOLOGY. NOW, IF YOU WOULD KINDLY CALL OFF THE LITTLE HOUNDS, MAYBE WE COULD WORK OUT A LONG-TERM SOLUTION TO YOUR ON-GOING PROBLEM?"

THE WOLF BELLOWED A SPECIAL DADDY *HOWL*

AWOOOOOO

AND THE CUBS SAT DOWN AND LOOKED AS HARMLESS AS PUPPIES.

TYLER QUICKLY PULLED HIS BROTHERS INTO AN EMERGENCY TEAM HUDDLE. A FEW MOMENTS LATER, THE SOUND OF HOOF SLAMS AND

"BREAK!"

WERE HEARD.
THE PIGS CAME OUT WITH A PROPOSITION FOR THE WOLF AND HIS YOUNG PACK.

"IF YOU EAT US NOW, YOU'LL JUST BE HUNGRY TOMORROW. BUT IF YOU AGREE TO BECOME A VEGETARIAN, WE WILL GIVE YOU HALF OF OUR FRUITS AND VEGETABLES EVERY WEEK."

THE WOLF SCRATCHED HIS UNCERTAIN HEAD...

"WAIT! THERE IS...ONE MORE THING," CONTINUED TREVOR.
"YOU HAVE TO STOP LURKING IN THE BUSHES
BY THE Puddle Pond Arena
AND SCARING THE HOCKEY TEAMS AND OUR FANIMALS AWAY."

THIS CAUSED THE WOLF A MOMENT FOR PAUSE...

THEY SEALED THE DEAL WITH A FEW HOOF-AND-PAW SHAKES.

THE WOLF AND THE "NO-PIG-OUT" ARRANGEMENT WAS GOING SMOOTHLY...

THE PIGS LEFT THE WOLF PART OF THEIR STOCK PILED HARVEST EVERY MONDAY - MORE THAN ENOUGH TO FEED A FAMILY OF TEN AND THE WOLF WAS NEVER SEEN AGAIN.

WELL, THAT IS, UNTIL ...

TWO WEEKS LATER,

DURING THE HABITAT CONFERENCE FINALS...

AS TYLER WAS ABOUT TO TAKE A SLAP SHOT FROM THE POINT, HE WAS SURPRISED TO SEE THE WOLF OVER IN HIS FAMILIAR BUSH.

HE WAS SO SHOCKED IN FACT, IT CAUSED HIM TO MISS THE PUCK ENTIRELY (WHICH *NEVER* HAPPENED TO *TYLER*).

TREVOR COULDN'T
BELIEVE HIS EYES!

"WHAT HAPPENED TYLER?
ARE YOU OKAY?
YOU LOOK A LITTLE RED.
HOW MANY HOOF PIGGIES
DO I HAVE UP?"

"I'M FINE, BUT I THINK 'LITTLE RED RIDING WOLF' IS GETTING TIRED OF EATING HIS VEGGIES!" SCREECHED TYLER. TREVOR LOOKED WHERE TYLER POINTED WITH HIS HOCKEY STICK AND SAW THE WOLF, IN HIS BEST DISGUISE YET, TRYING TO DUCK BACK BEHIND THE BUSH.

Gordie's Snack Shack

~~Chicken~~ Dinner
Veggie

Special! $9.99

"OH, THAT WOLF IS SKATING ON THIN ICE!"
EXCLAIMED TREVOR AS HE RACED OVER TO THE BUSHES...
FORGETTING
THAT
STOPPING ON
ICE SKATES
WASN'T HIS STRONGEST SKILL...

SLAM! * BAM!

WENT THE HAM!

TREVOR CRASHED RIGHT INTO THE BUSHES, THE WOLF
AND EVERYTHING IN BETWEEN.

THE OTHER PIG BROTHERS QUICKLY CAME SKATING TO HIS AID WHILE THEIR OPPONENTS, THE **CANADIAN BACONS,**

SCORED A... GOAL!

"YOU PROMISED NOT TO BOTHER US AGAIN," HUFFED AND PUFFED THE PIGS WITH HOCKEY STICKS RAISED IN THE AIR!

THE COW REFEREE BLEW HIS WHISTLE AND MOOED,

"NO HIGH STICKING!"

THAT UNSPORTSMANLIKE CONDUCT COST THE PIGS A TWO-MINUTE PENALTY AND POSSIBLY THE GAME.

"WE'LL WIN THE STANIMAL CUP WHEN PIGS FLY!
OUR NEXT OPPONENT, THE **PIGAGO BLACK HOGS**,
ARE A MUCH BETTER TEAM. THEY'RE GOING TO
SWEEP OUR PIG PEN AND TAKE US TO THE CLEANERS,"
SNORTED AN UNHAPPY MATTHEW.

"WELL, WITH AN ATTITUDE LIKE THAT, THEY MOST CERTAINLY WILL,"
SIGHED THE WOLF.

THE WOLF THOUGHT FOR A MOMENT BEFORE CONTINUING AND THEN SAID,

"I WOULD LIKE TO REPAY YOU FOR THE ABUNDANT FOOD YOU HAVE PROVIDED MY FAMILY.

HOW ABOUT I HELP YOU WITH YOUR HOCKEY?"

"WHAT COULD YOU POSSIBLY KNOW ABOUT HOCKEY?"
MATTHEW ASKED.

"WELL, THE LAST TIME I CHECKED THE SCOREBOARD, YOU STILL HAVEN'T WON *THIS* GAME," BEGAN THE WOLF BRAVELY.

"SO FOR STARTERS, TYLER, YOU HAVE AMAZING PUCK SKILLS AND FANCY FOOTWORK BUT DON'T FORGET - AN ASSIST IS JUST AS IMPORTANT AS A GOAL. IT'S ABOUT TEAMWORK! SOMETIMES YOU JUST NEED TO TRUST IN YOUR TEAMMATES TO TICKLE THE TWINE."

Habitat Conference Finals

THE MIGHTY PIGS — 2

Canadian Bacons — 3

LESSON no. 8

THE PIGS WERE NOT ONLY IMPRESSED BUT RELIEVED AS WELL.
THE WOLF HAD BEEN WATCHING THEM

AND **NOT** SIZING THEM UP
FOR HAM SANDWICHES
AFTER ALL.

"LASTLY, AND MOST IMPORTANTLY," SAID THE WOLF,

"NEVER GIVE UP -

THE GAME IS NOT OVER UNTIL THE COW BELL RINGS.

NOW GO OUT THERE, BELIEVE IN YOURSELF SO OTHERS WILL TOO. AND REMEMBER IT'S SUPPOSED TO BE FUN."

SO, THE PIGS DID JUST THAT;
THEY PUT FORTH THEIR BEST TEAM EFFORT AND
WON THE GAME!

THIS TIME, WHEN THE BENCHES CLEARED,
IT WAS FOR CELEBRATION IN TRUE
PIG-PILE STYLE!

AFTER THAT VICTORY, THEY ALL CAME TO A NEW AGREEMENT.

THE PIGS WOULD CONTINUE TO PROVIDE THE FRUITS, VEGGIES,

AND THE OCCASIONAL EGGS, AND IN TURN,

THE WOLF WOULD BE THEIR COACH.

AS THE WOLF TURNED AWAY HE SAID,

"OH, JUST CALL ME ... WOLF GREATSKY."

THAT's OUR DAD

THE PIGS' JAWS DROPPED, "THE GREAT ONE..."

WHISPERED THE THREE LITTLE PIGS IN AWE.

WOLF GREATSKY TOOK OVER AS HEAD COACH OF

THE NEW JERKEY MIGHTY PIGS

AND WITH A LOT OF DETERMINATION,

HEART,

AND A LITTLE PUCK LUCK,

THEY WENT ON TO WIN THE NEXT THREE STANIMAL CUPS!

AFTER HIS
RETIREMENT FROM COACHING,
THE WOLF REMAINED GOOD FRIENDS
WITH THE PIGS.

THEIR CUBS AND PIGLETS, FOR GENERATIONS TO COME,
ALL LIVED TOGETHER
HAPPILY EVER AFTER.